C0-FPZ-638

Surprised by a Cancer Diagnosis

Susan Melene Grittman

Surprised by a Cancer Diagnosis
Copyright © 2019 by Susan Melene Grittman

All Scripture quotations, unless noted otherwise, are taken from THE HOLY BIBLE, NEW INTERNATIONAL VERSION ®. Copyright © 1973, 1978, 1984 by International Bible Society. Used by permission of Zondervan Publishing House. All rights reserved.

All rights reserved. No part of this publication may be reproduced, stored in a retrieval system, or transmitted in any form or by any means – electronic, mechanical, photocopy, recording, or any other – except for brief quotations properly referenced in inspirational works or in printed reviews, without the prior permission of the AUTHOR/PUBLISHER.

ISBN - 9781728744025

Printed in the United States of America

DEDICATION:

To cancer patients, those who love them, and those who work for their healing

CONTENTS

INTRODUCTION

My guess is that you have opened this booklet because you (or a loved one) have begun a difficult journey due to a diagnosis of cancer or other life-threatening illness. If this is the case, you are likely overwhelmed and hardly know where and how to take the next step toward treatment, healing and wholeness.

When you receive such a diagnosis, it rocks your world and suddenly you are aware that your life is about to change. How do you go forward in the most life-giving way under the circumstances? A major life-threatening illness usually comes without warning. Therefore, we need support from others who have been through cancer or from those who have devoted their vocations to helping those who have cancer or other life-threatening illness.

I share this booklet with you in the hope that my experience and what I've learned will benefit you emotionally and spiritually and help prepare you for the journey ahead. This booklet is short – on purpose – so you will consider reading it first. Investing about thirty minutes to read this (and maybe longer to ponder) could be the best first step in your journey. Let these pages help you consider how you want to approach life in the midst of treatment. I encourage you to make some decisions that will help your perspective and attitude so you don't miss blessings and opportunities along the way. I was surprised by a cancer diagnosis, but I was more surprised by how much joy I discovered in the journey toward healing. My hope is that it will be the same for you. No matter your prognosis, no matter your circumstances or treatment plan, it is God's will to surprise you with joy in the journey. How does that sound?

MY STORY

I begin by sharing my story so you can have some context for the recommendations that I will offer. I have lived in the Houston area all my life and I know how to navigate life-threatening "rush" hour traffic on I-45. Ha! I have been through numerous hurricanes, so I know how to prepare for the tempest of a hurricane. More seriously, I am a pastor and have helped people prepare for death and funerals, so I have done some pre-planning for this major life event. But I was not prepared for a possible diagnosis of breast cancer. I had no advanced warning that I might have a health crisis, neither was I aware of any family history of breast cancer. I am a planner and like to live with the illusion that I am in control. I had no plan for cancer, and soon I would discover how much control I would have to surrender into the hands of the medical teams and insurance company who I needed to trust for my care.

What I had been preparing for was the birth of our first grandchild who was due in August. For years I had been telling my friends with grandchildren, "I was born to be a grandmother, and at the rate I am going I will never die!" I could not wait to hold this miracle from God in my arms. Immediately upon hearing the good news around Christmas time, I knew I wanted to have a "Grandma Day" once a week and was grateful we live close enough that this could be possible. At this stage in my life my work as an associate pastor was part-time and allowed me flexibility to set my own schedule, so I would be able to slip into my grandma role without rearranging my life. I had felt God's nudge leading me to plan my fall sermons and fall women's retreat messages ahead of the birth of the baby so that I could focus on being a grandmother. My husband and I prayed about the timing of our vacation and sensed that it would be OK to go in July if we were back three weeks ahead of the due date. We most certainly did not want to miss the big event. Prior to our vacation I planned the party we would have at our home at the end of August to welcome the new arrival. In addition, I had sensed God leading me to get all my yearly doctor appointments and screenings done before the baby arrived. By the time we left on vacation in early July, I had done as much advance planning as I could do and was ready for the big event.

A couple of days prior to vacation I had my yearly mammogram and ultrasound. When I saw the ultrasound I knew God was telling me that they would want to do a biopsy and I should not argue with them. (For years radiologists have been challenged to interpret my screenings, but God had led me to one of the best radiologists in the world, and I needed to trust the recommendation of the team.) The biopsy was scheduled for the day after we would return from vacation.

I was pretty sure God was preparing me for a cancer diagnosis. I praise God that I wasn't panicked. Through my history with God I know that His power and presence and the relationship He offers can bring Peace in the midst of life's "storms." (I have written about how I learned this in my book *Encountering the God of Surprises: Transformed by Joy.* You might find this a helpful resource for further reflection.)

My spirit was at peace, and I was experiencing a deep abiding trust in God. I felt no fear, only unsettled, as if my life was about to change. The timing seemed bad because I thought it would interfere with having quality time with my grandbaby. And then there was my busy schedule starting with the party, then the four sermons and women's retreat all happening before the end of October. Besides the uncertainty about being able to keep my present commitments and my concerns that I could be fully present for my family when needed, I felt a sense of loss – like I was aging and wouldn't be able to do what I used to do. I imagined what it would feel like for my appearance to change if I lost a breast.

I shared all of these concerns with the Lord and began to journal my thoughts. I noticed that the scripture printed on the page in my journal quoted Romans 8:28, "And we know that in all things God works for the good of those who love him, who have been called according to his purpose." I circled that, believing it was definitely true. Then I wrote:

> "What I know for sure is that some things do not change – that God is love, that God is present with me, that God desires to work in me and through me, that God gives good gifts in the midst of life's curve balls, that Jesus will always dance with me, that I am loved by many family and friends, and that each season has its own gifts. I will continue my Thanksgiving Journal, trust God, and live life to its full."

I prayed for God to heal me before the biopsy, knowing full well He could do that. But I sensed God telling me that I would go through treatment for healing the way most women do, and that He would use my experience to minister to others.

God's peace allowed me to put aside the thoughts about the probable diagnosis, and I thoroughly enjoyed our vacation. The day after we returned, I had the biopsy. The day after that our sweet Adeline was born 2 ½ weeks early. (Praise God we were back!) The following day I got the diagnosis of breast cancer. The cancer diagnosis did not overshadow the joy of the new life in our family!

After my husband and I met with the surgeon a few days later we learned that I had stage 1, estrogen-receptive positive, slow growing ductal carcinoma. It was small and the doctor did not expect me to need a mastectomy or chemotherapy. But because it had infiltrated outside the duct, I would likely need radiation in addition to a lumpectomy. I would likely be advised to take an estrogen suppressant for five years. I was concerned for what my moods might be like without hormones since I have had some history with emotional swings and even a period of depression in the past due to hormonal imbalance. The bad news was that I had cancer and the outcome was unknown.

The good news was that the cancer was treatable, and my heavenly Father had prepared the way for healing and I could see Him at work. I began making a long list of reasons for which I was thankful, for "God things" that had happened. For starters, I had my screening done early, and therefore the cancer was discovered sooner than it otherwise might have been. I already had the best surgeon in Spring, Texas. You might think I am not objective, but seriously almost every woman I knew in Spring who had been through surgery for breast cancer was singing Dr. Sutton's praises. He explained everything so well and even made a recording of the conversation for us to take home so we could hear it again, and he gave us his cell number in case we had more questions. Dr. Sutton recommended three oncologists, and one was Dr. Jenny Pozadzides at M.D. Anderson ~~Cancer~~ Center who my daughter, a nurse practitioner, had been referring patients to and felt good about. I was already a patient at M.D. Anderson because I get yearly skin cancer screenings, so God had prepared the way for me to feel confident in this choice and make it easy to get an appointment – the day after I called! And of course one of those things for which I was most grateful was that I had the joy of our new granddaughter. Such a gift!

A week after meeting with my surgeon, the meltdown happened. I could leave this part out of my story, but someone who has been recently diagnosed with a life-threatening condition needs to know that I can identify with your mixed emotions, and perhaps my honesty is what someone needs to help them cope. And someone may need to know what their recently diagnosed loved one may be going through so they can be a better support to them. One REALITY is that such news shakes your world. All of a sudden I was not coping very well. I did what I know usually helps me to cope. I found a place to be alone and began a journal entry. I wrote:

> "What it feels like to be me right now: Cancer? Really? I still feel healthy. But all that is about to change. A doctor is

going to cut off a part of my body. But that's not the worst. They are going to make me take meds I don't want to take that will give me side effects. I believe them – that this is for my good – to save my life. My life feels fragile. I feel old, vulnerable. I am fearful that I will not be myself ever again. I am afraid I will drive people away by my emotional state and confusion and fatigue. I am <u>already</u> tired. Overload! In one week I have had to digest medical terms and treatments and try to make good decisions about timing of treatment, doctors to use, and procedures to approve. My life depends on making good decisions, or at least my quality of life depends on making good decisions. I feel the weight of that. No one can make those decisions for me – but others will be affected by the decisions I make. I love my family and work, and I want to do my best by them. I am on a journey I did not choose. I feel out of control. I am angry in some ways. Not angry at anyone, not angry with God. Just wish I had some control, choice. I wish I could just be focused on the newest joy – Adeline. I want to have quality time with her and be able to keep her when her mom goes back to work – I don't want to be going through radiation and miss this! I am feeling disappointment, and I feel torn between medical self-care and emotional self-care (time to do things that are emotionally life-giving for me.) From what I have been reading, it is likely I will experience… [I made a list of side effects! But I'll leave that list out because it would not encourage the reader and some of what was on my list was not something I experienced anyway.] I need to cry. I don't want to need to cry… I am so tired. I don't want to think anymore. I need to turn my thoughts to the other REALITY – that God is at work!!"

As I was writing this my best friend, my clergy sister Pam, texted me and asked, "How are you doing?" It's miraculous how she reached out to me right at the time I needed prayer. As we say, "It's a God-thing." I called her and she listened and prayed in a way that helped me connect with God, the source of strength and hope. I had more clarity of thought after that, praise God! I had started to worry about things that might not happen. Thankfully, the meltdown only lasted a few hours. (If you are in meltdown mode right now, the Recommendations later in this booklet are there to help you through this.) The next morning in God's amazing personal way of intervention, I just happened to be listening to a song that was new to me, and I found joy and inspiration. This song would minister to me daily for weeks to come as I would listen to it on my morning walk. It reminded me that God sees every need that I have, that He is by my side no matter what I face, that He already knows what is up ahead on this journey I am on, that He will be my strength and comfort, and that He has good things in store for me in the midst of the struggle. I joined the author of the song in proclaiming that even when I don't yet see the answers for which I am praying, I can trust and will trust in God.

After I informed people of my diagnosis and asked for prayer, many people ministered to me. The prayer team at my church circled around me and prayed. They presented me with a prayer shawl that was crocheted by one of the members while praying for the one who would receive it. I felt wrapped in love from them and God. My Facebook friends' comments were overwhelming in sheer quantity and in their encouragement. One of my friends sent me a scripture she was praying for me from Colossians 1:11-12. "...being strengthened with all power according to his glorious might so that you may have great endurance and patience, and joyfully giving thanks to the Father who has qualified you to share in the inheritance of the saints in the kingdom of light." I loved how God placed that scripture on her heart to share with me. Stories of others who have fought cancer were an encouragement to me as well. Jane Maiers, a friend at my church, had cancer in her bile duct and liver. She was given a one percent chance of survival. Her vibrant faith carried her, and not only has she survived, she thrives! She serves God with great passion and joy. Capri, a clergywoman with whom I was acquainted, inspired me by the way she lived even though she was reportedly dying. I never saw her "dying" – I saw her *living* each day until she died. I wanted to be like these women, no matter the outcome of treatment. A former parishioner, Susan Precht, who lives with chronic pain had told me something that inspired me and I have never forgotten: "My pain does not define me. My attitude does. Luckily I get to pick my attitude." I wrote in my journal, "Joy is not dependent on my circumstances – I am not giving away my joy to cancer!" In the midst of cancer, I chose joy.

The day of surgery was approaching fast. I was so glad I would be able to get it over with quickly and start to heal before my daughter went back to work and needed help with Adeline. Because Adeline was born early, the party at our home was moved up and I could get that behind. But early in the morning on the day of the party I got very ill with fever and the stomach bug. We had to cancel the party – and the surgery. Of course I was disappointed on both accounts. On Facebook I posted:

> "'Lord, I will lift mine eyes to the hills knowing my help is coming from You. Your peace, You give me in time of the *storm*. You are the source of my strength. You are the strength of my life. I lift my hands in TOTAL PRAISE to you. Amen, Amen. Amen.' (lyrics from "Total Praise," italics mine) Today I cast out any fear, frustration or fatigue. I entrust all of me to God – again and again. With all the strength Jesus gives me, I hold his hand and we dance. (Maybe a slow dance – I promise not to overdo!) I love you all, and thank you for the prayers."

There is a story about a storm found in the Bible in Matthew 14:22-33. I saw the story in a new light because I was going through my own storm. The disciples of Jesus were caught in a storm on the Sea of Galilee while Jesus was still back on the land. It was night, and they were afraid and struggling. Jesus knew their need even though he could not see it with his eyes. He had no boat but nothing would prevent him from crossing in the storm to be present with his fearful disciples. He began to walk upon the water to them. The men thought they were seeing a ghost coming to them in the dark. Jesus called out, "Take heart, it is I; do not be afraid." One lesson is that if the Lord is with us we really don't need to be afraid! Jesus said so himself. This encouraged me, and I hope it will encourage you. Peter answered, "Lord, if it is You, command me to come to You on the water." "Come," says Jesus. Peter essentially asks Jesus to use him to prove that Jesus is who he claims to be. Is there a better request from a disciple? After the disciples know it is Jesus, after they witness both Jesus and Peter walking on water, and after Jesus commands the wind and it ceases, the disciples say, "Truly You are the Son of God." It was in a storm, in a place of danger and fear that the disciples recognized Jesus' divinity. Our storms become "opportunities" to draw closer to Jesus, to depend on God, and to build upon our history of trust in Him. My prayer was that God would use my experience to bring me closer to Him, to grow my faith, and to be a witness to others. God was bidding me "Come," and I was eager for God to use me to prove that Jesus is who He claims to be. I knew God was answering that prayer when a woman wrote me a note saying, "Your Peace, Faith and Joy are wonderful to witness. You are such an encouragement to any facing the same." I was praising God that he was using my life for His purposes and His glory, that He was present in such personal ways.

God provided for my surgery to be rescheduled one week later. Everything went well, and I was home the same day. I experienced God's peace and presence, and so did my husband. Now

I was gratefully enjoying the gifts of ice cream, Tiff's Treats, and my leftover family favorite of Chicken Spaghetti. Thankfully, I could resume coffee the next day! Reminds me of my daughter's wall hanging that says, "Every morning I need a little bit of coffee and a whole lot of Jesus."

Two days later we received the news of the pathology report. The edges were clear, meaning they got it all; the lymph nodes were clear, meaning no chemotherapy would be needed. It was anticipated that in two weeks I would have the follow up appointments – the follow-up with the surgeon and the oncology visit to discuss radiation options. Statistics show that there is a much greater chance that cancer will not return if radiation is done, but I didn't want radiation and didn't understand why I needed it if I was going to take a medicine that prevents the return of cancer. Mostly I didn't want to invest the time, and I didn't want the side effects.

One day prior to the scheduled doctor appointments, Hurricane Harvey's devastating, destructive, massive floodwaters began their assault on the Houston area. Our home was high and we were not flooded, but I wanted to help others. I was still healing from surgery and had to be careful not to overexert myself, and therefore I was frustrated that there was so little I could do to help. I was also frustrated that the appointments with the surgeon and radiation oncologist had to be postponed. I would have to wait for the follow up visit with my surgeon to find out why I had swelling developing in veins radiating from my incision. (Later this was diagnosed as a blood clot that would dissolve on its own, but at the time I was greatly concerned.) One of my doctors was stranded at the office, and no one could get in or out. Another couldn't get to the office. Both of their homes flooded. It made my problems seem so small. But for someone who is a planner like myself, living in chaos and not having a plan can be agony. I was going to have to be *patient* and *trust* God's timing for continued healing and radiation decisions.

On September 6 the flood waters had receded enough that my dedicated radiation oncologist, Dr. Pamela Schlembach, was able to meet with me and my husband for the discernment of the best protocol for treatment of my cancer. She explained that if breast cancer returns, it is usually in the same place. This helped me understand the recommendation for localized radiation. Later in the fall when radiation was complete, my radiation team paraded me down the hall, and I rang the bell. Tears formed from mixed emotions of gratitude and victory, but also from a realization of how fragile life is and how grateful I am to be alive. I was presented with a beautiful cotton washcloth crocheted by a volunteer. It was a joyful experience that evening to wash off the marks of radiation – no more visible signs or reminders of sickness left on my body. I had completed a major step toward healing, and that is all I wanted to "see."

Although I had had to scale back on some ministries and activities to make time for radiation, I had proclaimed in faith that I believed God was leading me to continue some ministries because He knew I could do it! I had enough energy to fulfill my commitment to preach in the midst of radiation treatments. I thank God for that! Although I was still tired from the healing that continued on the inside of my body from surgery and radiation, I was able to lead the women's retreat in October. The women celebrated with me that God had provided for this. And when my daughter went back to work at the beginning of November, I was able to begin "Grandma Day." God knew the desires of my heart and gifted me with this joy!

Following radiation, I was so ready to "move on" and forget about cancer. Unfortunately, that was not possible. As my body continued to heal from surgery and radiation I had some complications that required physical therapy. In addition, side effects from the cancer prevention medicine necessitated a medication change. I was grateful there was another medication option. The medical professionals that have the God-given spiritual gift of healing and who work diligently and compassionately to help others were God's provision throughout the journey of cancer treatments and helped me recover and be physically healthy.

The God of Surprises did not "surprise" me with cancer by His own hand – I know that God is not the author of disease. But God did allow the disease even though He could have healed it without surgery, radiation, physical therapy, and medication. Still, I find myself thanking God for the opportunity that I have had to grow through having breast cancer. Does that surprise you? It did me. I was surprised by a cancer diagnosis, but I was more surprised by how joyful I could feel in the midst of cancer. This was God's "Surprise!" Experiencing God's presence and guidance and seeing His provision all along the way was the source of joy that surpasses understanding.

My journey through cancer was much less difficult than it is for most people who have later stage cancer or need chemotherapy, yet it was still challenging and therefore an opportunity for introspection, growth in character, and trust in God. I discovered that while we experience some losses during such a difficult season, there are gains as well. From this experience we have new things to give such as the power of empathy, prayer and wisdom to offer others, a way to see life that makes our journey richer, and in my case, sharing my story to encourage others. I have mostly forgotten about the hard parts – it's not what I see. All I want to focus on is how God personally led me, sustained me, and blessed me with so many reasons to be thankful.

THANKSGIVING

Since thanksgiving keeps our perspective balanced and positive when we are going through a difficult season in life, I will share with you some of the reasons I found to be thankful, and I hope that it will encourage you to look for your own reasons to rejoice.

- God was so personal to minister to my spirit and teach me more about trust and surrender and patience.
- God prepared the way for me to have a great medical team.
- I never needed medication for mood swings – something for which I prayed fervently.
- I learned so much about cancer and treatments that it has filled me with new compassion for those with a diagnosis of cancer or other life-threatening illness.
- God led other women to me who needed encouragement who were going through similar experiences.
- It has been a good experience to be on the receiving end of much prayer and support. I feel like I am now a better pastor and friend to people going through life-threatening illness.
- I am thankful for the medical professionals who were God's instruments in such beautiful ways. Staff members at TOPS Comprehensive Breast Center and MD Anderson ~~Cancer~~ Center were professional, organized, always helpful, and patient. They not only understood my fears, confusion and questions, they anticipated these and were ready with help. The nurse navigators, RNs, aides, physical therapists, and doctors were huge blessings – all knowledgeable, kind, and dedicated. I am thankful for the lab technicians who offered warm-hearted conversation that distracted me from the discomfort of having to be stuck with a needle.
- I am thankful that I had insurance. Earlier this year on the phone with my nurse navigator from the insurance company, I told her that the insurance company helped save my life.
- I am thankful for Annie, the pharmacist at Walgreens, who took the time to address my questions – and offer encouragement and hope for no additional charge!

- I am thankful for researchers who develop the imaging technology and the protocols for treatment such as surgical procedures, radiation advancements, and the medications that are treating cancer patients.
- I am thankful for medical teachers and for students who devote themselves to years of study so they can help sick people. I am thankful for those who have been part of clinical trials in the past that have helped create new and better protocols. I am grateful to have the opportunity to "pay it forward" and be part of a clinical trial at MD Anderson which we believe is perfect for me and will help the medical profession do their best for their patients in the future.
- I am thankful for women who have had the courage to share their stories of their fight to beat breast cancer.
- I am thankful to the unseen volunteers who make tote bags, radiation smocks, washcloths, and more.
- I am thankful for the programs offered by the support groups which are so wonderful (and often fun) and make each person feel loved and beautiful even if they have lost their hair or they have reshaped bodies.
- I am thankful to God that I am a survivor and I CAN share my story.

I am thankful God led me to write and tell the story of my journey through cancer and healing so I can read it again and again and not take the gift of life for granted. I do not take it for granted that when I woke up this morning I had the health to play with my grandchild. I will not squander the gift of life that has been given me. I will live my life to the full and spread love and joy – all for God's glory.

I am thankful that God led me to tell my story if it can help others. I have prayed that how I tell my story will be an encouragement even to those who do not have a good prognosis for healing in this life. The good news is that no matter the prognosis we are not alone and can still find joy in the journey as we watch for God's surprises along the way. The best surprise still awaits all who love Him: When our bodies are too weak to continue, God has a plan to end our suffering, receive us into heaven into the arms of Love, and make us a new creation free from suffering.

It is my hope that how I tell my story will help you see God at work in your own life and help you find reasons to be thankful and praise God. Maybe you will tell *your* story to encourage others!

RECOMMENDATIONS

My hope for sharing my thoughts with you was to offer emotional and spiritual support, at least implicitly, through telling my story. But I want to be explicit in sharing with you some recommendations of things that helped me embrace life in the midst of cancer treatment.

First, get a blank notebook and begin listing everything you can think of for which you are thankful. Then *daily* add to the list at least one more reason you are thankful and grateful to be alive. I particularly like to record how I see God at work in my life. I also try to be aware of the tiny things that often go unnoticed yet come as a joyful surprise to my soul, such as seeing God's handiwork in creation when I noticed that the Monarch butterfly egg on my milkweed plant had hatched into a tiny caterpillar. My advice is not to miss or squander the treasures of the day by focusing on what is wrong. The daily discipline of thanks-living develops joy in the heart. Return thanks to God in prayer as you record your joys. Reread your list occasionally, especially when you are struggling emotionally.

Secondly, when you feel down, discouraged or overwhelmed, tell someone. You don't have to be on this journey on your own. Talk to a good listener. Talk to someone who will pray with you. Psychologists tell us that the number one thing to do when we are sinking into depression is to tell someone. This could be a friend, a medical professional, or a spiritual minister. Take advantage of nurse navigators who are available to you for no charge. I had nurse navigators at MD Anderson, TOPS Comprehensive Breast Center, and at my health insurance company. While all of these were helpful, two of these were also compassionate listeners and wonderful encouragers. I could privately share very personal medical and emotional concerns with someone objective, supportive, knowledgeable and well trained. Sometimes I would call them. Other times they called me.

Thirdly, reach out to God. Draw near to Him, bringing all your emotions and thoughts into the Light. Then Peace will begin to work in you and through you. I recommend that you go to God in prayer on a *daily* basis asking for God's strength and guidance. Be specific in speaking to God your needs and requests. This will help keep your eyes opened to see answers to prayer. As you see answers and see God working on your behalf, you can record those in your thanksgiving notebook. Additionally, I recommend attending worship weekly. God often spoke to me through the music, prayers, scripture, and community of faith-filled people.

If you are wrestling with questions of faith, if you are angry with God for allowing suffering and, in particular, *your* suffering, if you can't understand God's timing, or if what appears to be a lack of intervention on His part causes you to doubt his love and faithfulness – run TO Him – not away from Him. Do not shut Him out. You need Him now more than ever. Bring your questions, pain, anger, or disappointment to Him. Your Father already knows how you feel, and He is big enough to handle your emotions and questions. Tell Him! He can't heal what you try to hide from Him. One of my friends, Treva Kigor, suffered through a long period of spiritual wrestling before a Christian counselor helped her to voice her feelings to God. She learned that "God wants us to engage with Him in a conversation not just when we are happy but also when we are sad, confused, and even when we are angry. He can help us work through any feelings or situations we face."

A former parishioner and friend, Gary Zoch, shared with our Bible study class, "I have tried life with God, and I have tried life without God. It works better with God!" I am in agreement with Gary! I went through a devastating period earlier in my life where I shut God out. That is part of my history with God that I mentioned earlier. God reached out to me when I could not reach out to Him. I am so thankful! I went through cancer treatment *with* God, and it is my hope to help others find joy in a relationship with God that will sustain them through life's storms. So if you are struggling with questions of faith and need someone to talk to, feel free to contact me. In addition, I offer some resources (listed at the end of this booklet) that I have written on this subject and posted for download on my website.

Fourth on my list of recommendations for those with a life-threatening illness is to listen and sing along to beautiful, great music, especially music of your faith tradition. When I have been struggling to feel the joy, I put on Christian music and make myself sing. It's not easy for me to sing when I don't feel like it, meaning there is no song in my soul. But as an act of my will, if I put on Christian music and make myself sing, it transforms my soul. Pretty soon the beauty of the tune and instruments, the inspiration and truth of the lyrics, and the physical act of putting myself into the song, have lifted my spirit and changed my perspective to a more balanced one.

Fifthly, don't be afraid to ask for help. When someone says to you, "Call me if you need anything," take advantage of the offer! Pick up the phone and ask for help. If you need a ride to the doctor or lab for bloodwork, a few things from the grocery store or pharmacy, a serious conversation, or maybe just a friend to share lunch and talk about anything except the cancer, give your friend the opportunity to bless you. When we allow others to help us, they are equally blessed.

Lastly, soak up beauty wherever you can find it and do things that are life-giving for you. Some suggestions include spending time in nature such as walking, fishing, painting, reading, etc. Get outside on a beautiful day and photograph the surprises you find in nature. When weather does not permit this, look at pictures you have taken on vacations in beautiful places. Much of life's beauty is found in loving relationships, so take the initiative to invite people to join you as you feast on beauty. Perhaps look together at pictures and share memories of special times for which you are both thankful. Look into the faces of those who love you and care about your life and tell them how special they are to you. Plan ways to show your love and care for others. As you are able, help ease the struggle of someone else because as we do this, it is life-giving for ourselves as well.

It has been my prayer that my story, recommendations and resources will help support you and your loved ones if you find yourself on a difficult journey through a life-threatening illness. But my words pale in comparison to what *God* can do for you on this journey. So I offer this prayer to God on your behalf:

MY PRAYER: Gracious God, you know us and love us. You are with us at all times and have the power to calm a storm and calm a heart. You are a life-giving and healing God. You are our source of strength and joy. Not everyone knows this yet. Some who are reading my story may not know You at all. But it is You who have led them to my story. You desire for them to know they are loved, so I pray they will open their hearts to You and feel swallowed up in Your love for them. For those who are reading this who have a life-threatening condition, I pray that Your Spirit will guide them, minister to their needs, and increase their knowledge and trust in

You. Give them hope as You work to heal their bodies. Give them eyes to see You in the details and increase their awareness of the ways You work for good in the midst of all circumstances. May their experience be a source of inspiration for others. In Jesus' name. Amen.

Ringing the bell at the end of radiation treatments

Joy!

This picture represents to me my commitment to living the gift of each day to the full

RESOURCES
FOR ADDITIONAL REFLECTION AND SUPPORT

In years previous to my cancer diagnosis, I have struggled with questions of faith when life has thrown me curve balls. God answered my questions over time, and I have written the following short resources to help others with similar questions. They are available for download under "Resources" on my website: www.joyfullysusan.com.

- ***Why Do Bad Things Happen to God's People?*** This message gives examples and scripture to help the reader explore the complexity of the reasons people, even Christians, suffer.
- ***God's Response to Suffering*** This message helps the reader move beyond the "Why me?" question and open their eyes and heart to God who is compassionate, present and working on behalf of those who experience suffering of any type.
- ***Is God in Control? Reflections on the Sovereignty of God*** Do you struggle to understand how a God of love and power could be in control when the world is filled with so much suffering and evil? In this article I reflect on Scripture and show that "God is in control" but that "God is not controlling everything" – and why. There is a difference.

Visit joyfullysusan.com for additional resources and posts.

To chat or set up a speaking engagement please email me at susangrittman@gmail.com. It would be my joy to hear from you!

Also by Susan Grittman

Encountering the God of Surprises:

Transformed by Joy

ABOUT THE BOOK: In a transparent, touching, encouraging and easy-to-read conversational style, the author shares her stories of encounters with a very personal God. God reached into her heart full of grief, pain, and meaninglessness, transforming her with the joy of a new and vibrant personal relationship through Jesus Christ. The God of love invited her to partner with Him, and thus began an extra-ordinary adventure in a life of Christian ministry as a second career pastor while balancing family life with a husband and two children. It was nothing she expected but everything the God of surprises had dreamed for her. With honest and deeply personal story-telling, the author shares stories of healing, hope, struggles, disappointments, God-sized victories, and lessons learned through the journey.

Whether you are needing hope, wrestling with questions of faith, struggling to heal from pain or meaninglessness in your life, longing to grow closer to God, or needing new passion for ministry, this book will not disappoint and may even surprise you with your heart's desire.

Available at Amazon.com OR www.joyfullysusan.com